Cardboard House Press
www.cardboardhousepress.org
cardboardhousepress@gmail.com

CADAVERS / CADÁVERES
Copyright © 2018 Roberto Echavarren
Translation © 2018 Roberto Echavarren and Donald Wellman
Cover image and interior graphics © 2018 Yudi Yudoyoko

Designed by Mutandis
mutandisdesign@gmail.com

First Edition, 2018
Printed in the United States of America

ISBN 978-1-945720-10-9
Distributed by Small Press Distribution

Cardboard House Press is a 501c3 nonprofit organization devoted to the creation
of spaces and media for cultural, artistic, and literary development through the
publication and circulation of writing, art, and contemporary thought from
Latin America and Spain and through bilingual events, community projects
and workshops. Our work serves as a platform to exchange ideas and highlight
meanings that stimulate diverse human connections and social actions.

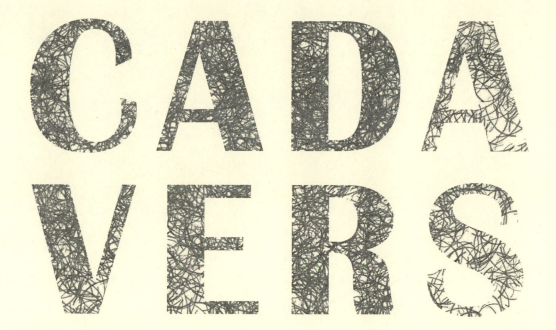

CADAVERS

NÉSTOR PERLONGHER

TRANSLATED BY ROBERTO ECHAVARREN AND DONALD WELLMAN

Bajo las matas
En los pajonales
Sobre los puentes
En los canales
Hay Cadáveres

En la trilla de un tren que nunca se detiene
En la estela de un barco que naufraga
En una olilla, que se desvanece
En los muelles los apeaderos los trampolines los malecones
Hay Cadáveres

En las redes de los pescadores
En el tropiezo de los cangrejales
En la del pelo que se toma
Con un prendedorcito descolgado
Hay Cadáveres

En lo preciso de esta ausencia
En lo que raya esa palabra
En su divina presencia
Comandante, en su raya
Hay Cadáveres

En las mangas acaloradas de la mujer del pasaporte que se arroja
por la ventana del barquillo con un bebito a cuestas
En el barquillero que se obliga a hacer garrapiñada

Under the brush
In the scrub
Upon the bridges
In the canals
There Are Cadavers

In the chug of a train that will not desist
In the wake of a boat that runs aground
In a wavelet, that vanishes
On the wharves loading docks trampolines piers
There Are Cadavers

In the nets of fishermen
In the tumbling of crayfish
In she whose hair is nipped
by a small loose hairclip
There Are Cadavers

In the preciseness of this absence
In that which erases the word
In your divine presence
Commander, in your hair line
There Are Cadavers

In the warmed-up sleeves of the passport woman who throws
herself through the window of the little boat with a baby in her arms
In the wafer man committed to making candied nuts

En el garrapiñero que se empana
En la pana, en la paja, ahí
Hay Cadáveres

Precisamente ahí, y en esa richa
de la que deshilacha, y
en ese soslayo de la que no conviene que se diga, y
en el desdén de la que no se diga que no piensa, acaso
en la que no se dice que se sepa...
Hay Cadáveres

Empero, en la lingüita de esa zapato que se lía, disimuladamente, al
        espejuelo, en la
correíta de esa hebilla que se corre, sin querer, en el techo, patas
arriba de ese monedero que se deshincha, como un buhón, y, sin
embargo, en esa c... que, cómo se escribía? c... de qué?, mas, Con
        Todo
Sobretodo
Hay Cadáveres

En el tapado de la que se despelmaza, febrilmente, en la
menea de la que se lagarta en esa yedra, inerme en el
despanzurrar de la que no se abriga, apenas, sino con un
saquito, y en potiche de saquitos, y figurines anteriores, modas
pasadas como mejas muertas de las que
Hay Cadáveres

Se ven, se los despanza divisantes flotando en el pantano:
en la colilla de los pantalones que se enchastran, símilmente;

In the candied nut cart that is dusted with sugar pieces
In the corduroy, in the straw, right there
There Are Cadavers

Precisely there, in that skein
which she unravels, and
in that turning aside of she who need not be mentioned,
in the disdain of she whom we must not say she doesn't think, perhaps
in she of whom it is not said that she knows…
There Are Cadavers

Nevertheless, in the tongue of that shoe that is tied, slyly, to
          the hand mirror, in the
thin strap that is fastened, by accident, on the ceiling, feet
up of this purse that deflates like an owl, and,
nonetheless, in that c… what, how was it spelled? c… of what? but, All
          In all
Above all
There Are Cadavers

In the coat belonging to she who lies down feverishly, in the
hobble of she who lizards herself in that ivy, vulnerable, in the
disembowelment of she who doesn't wrap herself up, barely, except in a
woolen jacket, and in a pile of little jackets, and out-of-date fashion sketches, fashions
like dead cast-offs of which
There Are Cadavers

They can be seen, eviscerated, floating in the bog;
in the seats of dirtied pants, similarly;

en el ribete de la cola del tapado de seda de la novia, que no se casa
porque su novio ha
……………………..!
Hay Cadáveres

En ese golpe bajo, en la bajez
de esa mofleta, en el disfraz
ambiguo de ese buitre, la zeta de
esas azaleas, encendidas, en esa obscuridad
Hay Cadáveres

Está lleno: en los frasquitos de leche de chancho con que las campesinas
agasajan sus fiólos, en los
fiordos de las portuarias y marítimas que se dejan amanecer, como a
        escondidas, con la bombacha llena; en la
humedad de esas bolsitas, bolas, que se apisonan al movimiento de
        los de
Hay Cadáveres

Parece remanido: en la manea
de esos gauchos, en el pelaje de
esa tropa alzada, en los cañaverales (paja brava), en el botijo
de ese guacho, el olor a matorra de ese juiz
Hay Cadáveres

Ay, en el quejido de esa corista que vendía "estrellas federales"
Uy, en el pateo de esa arpista que cogía pequeños perros invertidos,
Uau, en el peer de esa carrera cuando rumbea la cascada, con
una botella de whisky "Russo" llena de vidrio en los breteles, en ésos,

in the trim of the train of the silk coat worn by the bride, who doesn't marry
because the groom has
.....................!
There Are Cadavers

In that low blow, in the lowness
of that chubby cheek, in the ambiguous
disguise of that vulture, the *zeta* of
those azaleas, shining brightly, in that darkness
There Are Cadavers

It's full of them: in the little flasks of pig milk which country girls
lavish on their pimps, in the fjords
where port and maritime girls remain until dawn, as if
        hidden, with their baggy pants full; in the
moisture of those little bags, balls, that are flattened by the moving
        of those from
There Are Cadavers

It seems obvious: in the hobble
of those gauchos, in the fur
of that rebel troop, in the reedbeds (wild hay), in the booty
of that boy, in the stench of that judge's pubic hair
There Are Cadavers

Ay, in the moan of that chorus girl who sold "federal badges"
Uh, in the kicking of that harpist who fucked queer dogs,
Woof, in the farting of that run toward the waterfall, with a
bottle of "Russo" whisky full of shattered glass in the straps, in those,

tan delgados,
Hay Cadáveres

En la finura de la modistilla que atara cintas do un buraco hubiere
En la delicadeza de las manos que la manicura que electriza
las uñas salitrosas, en las mismas
cutículas que ella abre, como en una toilette; en el tocador, tan
...indeciso..., que
clava preciosamente los alfiles, en las caderas de la Reina y
en los cuadernillos de la princesa, que en el sonido de una realeza
que se derrumba, oui
Hay Cadáveres

Yes, en el estuche de alcanfor del precho de esa
¡bonita profesora!
Ecco, en los tizones con que esa ¡bonita profesora! traza el rescoldo
de ese incienso;
Da, en la garganta de esa ajorca, o en lo mollejo de ese moretón
atravesado por un aro, enagua, en
Ya
Hay Cadáveres

En eso que empuja
lo que se atraganta,
En eso que traga
lo que emputarra,
En eso que amputa
lo que empala,

so thin,
There Are Cadavers

In the daintiness of the little seamstress who attached ribbons where a hole might have been
In the delicacy of the manicured electrolyzed hands with
salty nails, in the very
cuticles she trims, in her toilette; in the dressing table, so
… uncertain ….
she inserts pins fitfully, in the hips of the Queen and
in the little notebooks of the princess, with the noise of a crumbling
royalty, oui
There Are Cadavers

Yes, in the camphor box on the chest of that
pretty teacher!
Ecco, in the charred sticks with which that pretty teacher! sketches the embers
of that incense;
Da, in the throat of that necklace, or in the softness of that bruise
crossed by a hoop, a petticoat, in
Already
There Are Cadavers

In that which pushes
what chokes,
In that which swallows
what fucks,
In that which severs
what impales,

En eso que ¡puta!
Hay Cadáveres

Ya no se puede sostener: el mango
de la pala que clava en la tierra su rosario de musgos,
el rosario
de la cruz que empala en el muro la tierra de una clava,
la corriente
que sujeta a los juncos el pichido - tin, tin... - del sonajero,
en el gargajo que se esputa...
Hay Cadáveres

En la mucosidad que se mamosa, además, en la gárgara; en la también
glacial amígdala; en el florete que no se succiona con fruición
porque guarda una orla de caca; en el escupitajo
que se estampa como sobre en un pijo,
en la saliva por donde penetra un elefante, en esos chistes de
la hormiga,
Hay Cadáveres

En la Conchita de las pendejas
En el pitín de un gladiador sureño, sueño
En el florín de un perdulario que se emparrala, en unas
brechas, en el sudario del cliente
que paga un precio desmesuradamente alto por el polvo,
en el polvo
Hay Cadáveres

In that which, shit!
There Are Cadavers

It can no longer be upheld: the handle
of the shovel that nails into the earth its rosary of moss,
the rosary
of the cross that impales on the wall the earth of a pike,
the current
that ties the reeds to the pitch – tin tin… of the rattle
in the phlegm that's spewed…
There Are Cadavers

In the mucus that is suckled, in the gargle also; in the also
glacial amygdala: in the foil that is not suckled with fruition
because it has an edge of shit; in the spittle
that's stamped on a dick,
in the saliva by which an elephant penetrates, in those ant
jokes,
There Are Cadavers

In the Pussy of the sluts
In the wee-wee of a southern gladiator, I dream
In the florin of a dissolute who opens his legs, in some
breaches, in the shroud of the client
who pays an exorbitantly high price for a quickie
in the quickie
There Are Cadavers

En el desierto de los consultorios
En la polvareda de los divanes "inconcientes"
En lo incesante de ese trámite, de ese "proceso" en hospitales
donde el muerto circula, en los pasillos
donde las enfermeras hacen SHHH! con una aguja en los ovarios,
en los huecos
de los escaparates de cristal de orquesta donde los cirujanos
se travisten de "hombre drapeado",
laz zarigüeyaz de dezhechoz, donde tatúase, o tajéase (o paladea)
un paladar, en tornos
Hay Cadáveres

En las canastas de mamá que alternativamente se llenan o vacían de
esmeraldas, canutos, en las alforzas de ese
bies que ciñe - algo demás - esos corpinos, en el azul lunado del cabello,
gloriamar, en el chupazo de esa teta que se exprime, en el
reclinatorio, contra una mandolina, salamí, pleta de tersos caños...
Hay Cadáveres

En esas circunstancias, cuando la madre se
lava los platos, el hijo los pies, el padre el cinto, la
hermanita la mancha de pus, que, bajo el sobaco, que
va "creciente", o
Hay Cadáveres

Ya no se puede enumerar: en la pequeña "riela" de ceniza
que deja mi caballo al fumar por los campos (campos, hum...), o por
los harás, eh, harás de cuenta de que no
Hay Cadáveres

In the desert of the doctor's office
In the quickies on "unconscious" divans
In the incessant goings on of that "process" in hospitals
where the dead roam around, in the hallways
where the nurses go SHHH! with a needle in their ovaries,
in the hollows
of glass orchestra showcases where surgeons
cross-dress as a "draped man,"
the possumz in ze garbage, where a palate is tattooed, or slashed (or relishes),
in lathes
There Are Cadavers

In mama's baskets that alternatively are emptied or filled
with emeralds, tubes, in the tuck
of that bias that tightens – a little too much – those bras, in the moony blue hair
seaglory, in the sucking of that squeezed tit, in
the kneeling stool, against a mandolin, salami, pool of smooth pipes
There Are Cadavers

Under those circumstances, when the mother
washes the dishes, the son his feet, the father his belt, the little
sister a spot of pus that, beneath the armpit,
keeps "waxing," or
There Are Cadavers

It cannot be enumerated any longer: in the little "glint" of ash
my horse drops as it smokes across the fields (fields, ahem…), or in the stud farms,
eh, because you will pretend that no
There Are Cadavers

Cuando el caballo pisa
los embonchados pólderes,
empenachado se hunde
en los forrajes;
cuando la golondrina, tera tera,
vola en circuitos, como un gallo, o cuando la bondiola
como una sierpe "leche de cobra" se
disipa,
los miradores llegan todos a la siguiente
conclusión:
Hay Cadáveres

Cuando los extranjeros, como crápulas, ("se les ha volado la
papisa, y la manotean a dos cuerpos"), cómplices,
arrodíllanse (de) bajo la estatua de una muerta,
y ella es devaluada!
Hay Cadáveres

Cuando el cansancio de una pistola, la flacidez de un ano,
ya no pueden, el peso de un carajo, el pis de un
"palo borracho", la estirpe real de una azalea que ha florecido
roja, como un seibo, o un servio, cuando un paje
la troncha, calmamente, a dentelladas, cuando la va embutiendo
contra una parecita, y a horcajadas, chorrea, y
Hay Cadáveres

Cuando la entierra levemente, y entusiasmado por el suceso
de su pica, más
atornilla esa clava, cuando "mecha"

When the horse steps over
muddy polders,
and crested, sinks
into the fodder;
when the swallow, "tera tera,"
flies in circuits like a rooster, or when the pig
like a "cobra milk" serpent
evaporates,
lookers-on at home all come to the following
conclusion:
There Are Cadavers

When foreigners like reprobates ("the female pope has
flown away, they try to snatch her with two bodies"), conspiratorial,
kneel (be-) low under the statue of a dead woman,
and she is devalued!
There Are Cadavers

When the weariness of a gun, the flabbiness of an asshole,
are no longer able, the weight of a cock, the piss from a
"drunken prick," the royal lineage of an azalea that has flowered
red, like the silk-cotton tree, or a Serbian, when a page
cuts it off calmly with a snap of the teeth, when he crams it
against a low wall, astraddle, it drips, and
There Are Cadavers

When he buries it lightly, and enthralled by the incident
of his lance,
he screws that bludgeon further, when he "stuffs"

en el pistilo de esa carroña el peristilo de una carroza
chueca, cuando la va dándola vuelta
para que rase todos... los lunares, o
Sitios,
Hay Cadáveres

Verrufas, alforranas (de teflón), macarios muermos: cuando sin...
acribilla, acrisola, ángeles miriados de peces espadas, mirtas
acneicas, o sólo adolescentes, doloridas del
dedo de un puntapié en las várices, torreja
de ubre, percal crispado, romo clít...
Hay Cadáveres

En el país donde se yuga el molinero
En el estado donde el carnicero vende sus lomos, al contado,
y donde todas las Ocupaciones tienen nombre...
En las regiones donde una piruja voltea su zorrito de banlon,
la huelen desde lejos, desde antaño
Hay Cadáveres

En la provincia donde no se dice la verdad
En los locales donde no se cuenta una mentira—
Esto no sale de acá—
En los meaderos de borrachos donde aparece una pústula roja en
la bragueta del que orina—esto no va a parar aquí—, contra los
azulejos, en el vano, de la 14 o de la 15, Corrientes y
Esmeraldas,
Hay Cadáveres

in the pistil of that carrion the peristyle of a crooked
carriage, and makes it turn
to raze all …. the birthmarks, or
Spots,
There Are Cadavers

Warts, hemorrhoids (of teflon), farcy Macario: when without …
strafes, makes transparent, angels endowed with swordfishes, acned
Mirtas, or just adolescent girls, their fingers
sore from the kick in the varicose veins, French toast
of udders, crisp percale, blunt clit …
There Are Cadavers

In the country where they yoke the miller
In the state where the butcher sells his roasts, for cash,
and where all Occupations have a name …
In the regions where a hooker turns over her fox fur of banlon
they smell her from afar, from long ago
There Are Cadavers

In the province where they don't tell the truth
In the bars where they don't tell a lie—
It is strictly among us—
In the urinals of drunkards where a red pustule appears
in the fly of one who pisses—this will not stop here – against
the tiles, at the door, of fourteen or fifteen, Corrientes Avenue
and Esmeralda Street,
There Are Cadavers

Y se convierte inmediatamente en La Cautiva,
los caciques le hacen un enema,
le abren el c... para sacarle el chico,
el marido se queda con la nena,
pero ella consigue conservar un escapulario con una foto borroneada,
de un camarín donde...
Hay Cadáveres

Donde él la traicionó, donde la quiso convencer que ella
era una oveja hecha rabona, donde la perra
lo cagó, donde la puerca
dejó caer por la puntilla de boquilla almibarada unos pelillos
almizclados, lo sedujo,
Hay Cadáveres

Donde ella eyaculó, la bombachita toda blanda, como sobre
un bombachón de muñequera, como en
un cáliz borboteante - los retazos
de argolla flotaban en la "Solución Humectante"
                                        (método agua por agua),
ella se lo tenía que contar:
Hay Cadáveres

El feto, criándose en un arroyuelo ratonil,
La abuela, afeitándose en un bols de lavandina,
La suegra, jalándose unas pepitas de sarmiento,
La tía, volviéndose loca por unos peines encurvados:
Hay Cadáveres

And she immediately turns into La Cautiva,
the caciques give her an enema,
they open her c… to take out the child,
the husband keeps the girl,
but she keeps holding onto a scapula with a worn-out photo,
of an alcove where …
There Are Cadavers

Where he betrayed her, where he tried to convince her that she
was a lamb with a short tail, where the bitch
shit on him, where the hog
shed by the tip of the syrupy mouthpiece
musky little hairs, and seduced him
There Are Cadavers

Where she ejaculated, her panties all soft, like a
doll's baggy bloomers, as in
a bubbling chalice—the shreds
of a shackle floated in the "Moisture Solution"
                                    (method water by water),
she had to tell him:
There Are Cadavers

The fetus, growing in a rat-infested sewer,
The grandmother, shaving herself in a bowl of bleach,
The mother-in-law, guzzling a few seeds of vine shoot,
The aunt, going crazy for some ornamental combs:
There Are Cadavers

La familia, hurgándolo en los repliegues de las sábanas
La amiga, cosiendo sin parar el desgarrón de una "calada"
El gil, chupándose una yuta por unos papelitos desleídos
Un chongo, cuando intentaba introducirla por el caño de escape de una Kombi,
Hay Cadáveres

La despeinada, cuyo rodete se ha raído
por culpa de tanto "rayito de sol", tanto "clarito";
La martinera, cuyo corazón prefirió no saberlo;
La desposeída, que se enganchó los dientes al intentar huir de un taxi;
La que deseó, detrás de una mantilla untuosa, desdentarse
para no ver lo que veía:
Hay Cadáveres

La matrona casada, que le hizo el favor a la muchacho pasándole un buen punto;
la tejedora que no cánsase, que se cansó buscando el punto bien
      discreto que no mostrara nada
      y al mismo tiempo diera a entender lo que pasase—;
      la dueña de la fábrica, que vio las venas de sus obreras urdirse
táctilmente en los telares - y daba esa textura acompasada...
                                    lila...
La lianera, que procuró enroscarse en los hilambres, las púas
Hay Cadáveres

La que hace años que no ve una pija
La que se la imagina, como aterciopelada, en una cuna (o cuña)
Beba, que se escapó con su marido, ya impotente, a una quinta
      donde los
vigilaban, con un naso, o con un martillito, en las rodillas, le

The family, rummaging for him in the folds of the sheets
The friend, sewing non-stop a "run" in her stocking
The jerk, sucking a blackjack in exchange for some faded papers,
A jackass, when trying to stick it inside the exhaust pipe of a van,
There Are Cadavers

The disheveled woman, whose bun became frayed
due to so many "rays of sun," to so much "bleaching;"
the Martinera whose heart chose to ignore it;
the dispossessed woman, who hooked her teeth when attempting to flee from a taxi;
the one who preferred, from behind an unctuous mantilla, to pull her teeth out
so as not to see what she saw:
There Are Cadavers

The married matron, who did the boy a favor by passing him a good point;
The tireless weaver, who tired herself out seeking the cautious stitch
        that wouldn't reveal anything
        and at the same time would insinuate what was going on— :
        the factory owner, who saw the veins of her workers weaving
palpably through the looms—and gave that regular texture …
                                        lilac …
The spinner, who managed to coil herself in the wires, in the barbs
There Are Cadavers

She who hasn't seen a dick in years
She who imagines it, velvety, in a cradle (or a wedge)
Beba, who escaped with her husband, already impotent, to a villa
        where they
watched them, with a schnoz or a small hammer, on the knees, they

tomaron los pezones, con una tenacilla (Beba era tan bonita como una profesora...)
Hay Cadáveres

Era ver contra toda evidencia
Era callar contra todo silencio
Era manifestarse contra todo acto
Contra toda lambida era chupar
Hay Cadáveres

Era: "No le digas que lo viste conmigo porque capaz que se dan cuenta"
O: "No le vayas a contar que lo vimos porque a ver si se lo toma a pecho"
Acaso: "No te conviene que lo sepa porque te amputan una teta"
Aún: "Hoy asaltaron a una vaca"
"Cuando lo veas hace de cuenta que no te diste cuenta de nada...
        y listo"
Hay Cadáveres

Como una muletilla se le enchufaba en el pezcuello
Como una frase hecha le atornillaba los corsets, las fajas
Como un titilar olvidadizo, eran como resplandores de mangrullo, como
una corbata se avizora, pinche de plata, así
Hay Cadáveres

En   el campo
En el campo
En la casa
En la caza
Ahí
Hay Cadáveres

grabbed her nipples with some little pincers (Beba was as pretty as a teacher…)
There Are Cadavers

It was to see despite all evidence
It was to fall silent against all silence
It was to protest against every act
Against all licking to suck
There Are Cadavers

It was: "Don't tell him you saw me with him, since they might realize"
Or: "Don't go telling him what we saw, since he might take it to heart"
Perhaps: "It's no good for him to know, since they'll hack off one of your tits"
Still: "Today they mugged a cow"
"When you see him pretend not to notice…
        that's it"
There Are Cadavers

Like a pet phrase plugged into his neck
Like a hackneyed phrase tightening the corsets, the girdles
Like a forgetful shimmer, like a gleaming catfish, like
a necktie half seen, clasp of silver, like that
There Are Cadavers

In   the field
In the field
In the house
In the hunt
There
There Are Cadavers

En el decaer de esta escritura
En el borroneo de esas inscripciones
En el difuminar de estas leyendas
En las conversaciones de lesbianas que se muestran la marca de la liga,
En ese puño elástico,
Hay Cadáveres

Decir "en" no es una maravilla?
Una pretensión de centramiento?
Un centramiento de lo céntrico, cuyo forward
muere al amanecer, y descompuesto de
El Túnel
Hay Cadáveres

Un área donde principales fosas?
Un loro donde aristas enjauladas?
Un pabellón de lolas pajareras?
Una pepa, trincada, en el cubismo de superficie frivola...?

Hay Cadáveres

Yo no te lo quería comentar, Fernando, pero esa vez que me mandaste
        a la oficina a hacer los trámites, cuando yo
cruzaba la calle, una viejita se cayó, por una biela, y los
carruajes que pasaban, con esos crepés tan anticuados (ya preciso,
        te dije, de otro pantalón blanco), vos crees que
        se iban a detener, Fernando? Imagina...
Hay Cadáveres

In the collapse of this writing
In the blurring of those inscriptions
In the blending of these legends
In the conversations of lesbians who display the marks left by their garters.
In that elastic fist,
There Are Cadavers

To say "in," isn't it a marvel?
An attempt at centering?
A centering of the central, whose forward
dies at dawn and decomposes by
The Tunnel
There Are Cadavers

A zone where principal graves?
A parrot where caged edges?
A pavilion of tits inside birdcages?
A cunt, tied up, in the cubism of a frivolous surface…?

There Are Cadavers

I didn't want to mention it, Fernando, but that time you sent me
        to the office to do the paperwork, while I
was crossing the street, a little old woman fell down, hit by a piston rod, and
the carriages going by, with those outdated crepes (I happen to need,
        as I've told you, another pair of white pants) do you think
        they were going to stop, Fernando? Just imagine …
There Are Cadavers

Estamos hartas de esta reiteración, y llenas
de esta reiteración estamos.
Las damiselas italianas
pierden la tapita del Luis XV en La Boca!
Las "modelos" - del partido polaco -
no encuentran los botones (el escote cerraba por atrás) en La Matanza!
Cholas baratas y envidiosas - cuya catinga no compite - en Quilmes!
Monas muy guapas en los corsos de Avellaneda!
Barracas!
Hay Cadáveres

Ay, no le digas nada a doña Marta, ella le cuenta al nieto que es colimba!
Y si se entera Misia Amalia, que tiene un novio federal!
Y la que paya, si callase!
La que bordona, arpona!
Ni a la vitrolera, que es botona!
Ni al lustrabotas, cachafaz!
Ni a la que hace el género "volante"!
NI
Hay Cadáveres

Féretros alegóricos!
Sótanos metafóricos!
Pocilios metonímicos!
Ex—plícito!
Hay Cadáveres

Ejercicios
Campañas

We are sick of this reiteration, and full
of this reiteration we are.
The Italian damsels
lose the lid of the Louis the XV in La Boca!
The "models" – of the Polish party –
cannot find the buttons (the low-cut dress fastened from behind) in La Matanza!
Cheap envious half-castes – whose stink doesn't compete – in Quilmes!
Very pretty chicks on the floats in Avellaneda!
Barracas!
There Are Cadavers

Ay! Don't tell anything to Doña Marta, she tells her grandson who's been drafted!
And if Donna Amalia finds out, who has a boyfriend in the army!
And the one who talks big, if only she'd shut up!
She who plays the bourdon is a harpy!
Nor to the phonograph player, she's a police informer!
Nor to the bootblack, the rascal!
Nor to she who weaves the "flying" cloth!
NOR
There Are Cadavers

Allegorical coffins!
Metaphorical basements!
Metonymical teacups!
Ex—plicit!
There Are Cadavers

Exercises
Campaigns

Consorcios
Condominios
Contractus
Hay Cadáveres

Yermos o Luengos
Pozzis o Westerleys
Rouges o Sombras
Tablas o Pliegues
Hay Cadáveres

—Todo esto no viene así nomás
—Por qué no?
—No me digas que los vas a contar
—No te parece?
—Cuándo te recibiste?
—Militaba?
—Hay Cadáveres?

Saliste Sola
Con el Fresquito de la Noche
Cuando te Sorprendieron los Relámpagos
No Llevaste un Saquito
Y
Hay Cadáveres

Se entiende?
Estaba claro?
No era un poco demás para la época?

Consortiums
Condominiums
Contracts
There Are Cadavers

Barren or long
Pozzis or Westerleys
Rouges or Shadows
Pleats or Folds
There Are Cadavers

—All of this doesn't happen just so
—Why not?
—Don't tell me you're going to count them
—Don't you think so?
—When did you graduate?
—Was he a member of?
—Are there cadavers?

You Went out Alone
In the Freshness of the Night
When the Lightning Took you by Surprise
You Didn't wear a Woolen Jacket
And
There Are Cadavers

Is it understood?
Was it clear?
Wasn't it a little too much for the times?

Las uñas azuladas?
Hay Cadáveres

Yo soy aquél que ayer nomás...
Ella es la que...
Veíase el arpa...
En alfombrada sala...
Villegas o
Hay Cadáveres

……………………………
……………………………
……………………………
……………………………

No hay nadie?, pregunta la mujer del Paraguay.
Respuesta: No hay cadáveres.

Bluish fingernails?
There Are Cadavers

I am the one who only yesterday…
She is the one who…
You could see the harp…
In the carpeted lounge…
Villegas or
There Are Cadavers

……………………………
……………………………
……………………………
……………………………

There's no one here? the woman from Paraguay asks.
Answer: There are no cadavers.

This is the best known poem by Néstor Perlongher. It belongs to his second book, *Alambres* (1987). It alludes to the genocide in Argentina in the seventies, during the military dictatorship. It's an overwhelming subject, even if we only think of the number of victims (thirty thousand). But "Cadavers" is not only about the murders. It combines and contrasts two lines of development: the political and the erotic. To the insistent refrain, "Hay cadáveres," which threads the entire poem, the verses respond with a proliferation of signifiers that elude the censorship the authorities would have liked to impose. The refrain is an alarm, a call for attention. It threads the stanzas and gives them a rhythm. It insists on something that official truth refuses to admit. It is terminally sinister, like Poe's "Nevermore." Now, where are those cadavers? Everywhere: in the sea, in the countryside, in the cities, in the neighborhoods of Buenos Aires (Quilmes, Avellaneda, Barracas). They impregnate clothes, mix with body secretions, stick to the officers' heads of hair as if they were lice. The poem intones a murmur, a rumor, a hearsay, a clandestine under-clad notion, the all-pervading atmosphere of genocide. But the verses run according to their own bent, often associating words by phonic similitude. They are the verve of intimate colloquial utterance with erotic, funny and sinister implications, and exploit the color and double entendre of street language expressions, the suggestive power of incomplete sentences, allusions, hints, altered words. It's a live language that operates on its own, a testimony about death but also a creation of poetic texture. The jocose tone might seem upsetting, considering the gravity of the subject matter. However, the poem doesn't merely deal with a political reality. By a radical turnabout, it makes politics inhabit the poem. The sandwiched stanzas encompass erotic encounters, sexual allusions among a variety of popular characters belonging to the mainstream. They form a web of entangled desires, pleasures, conflicts with humorous effect. Its inventive proliferation goes beyond the fact that there are cadavers. While the refrain doesn't stop naming them, the verses produce a chain of interlocked combinations revealing a genetic disorder where something closeted mutters, whispers salacious lustful lecherous comments sometimes in the form of a question, or a broken sentence. The tone is playful and mannered, reminiscent of the way of speaking of a poof or effeminate homosexual. One should keep in mind that this disheveled discourse was considered a menace by the authorities; it was censored and punished by the male chauvinistic dictatorship. This accounts for the interplay between desire and furtiveness within the cluster of ambiguous connotations, a secret language among initiates, expressions coming from lunfardo or gaucho dialects, or the vocabulary of dressmakers and hairdressers. Obscene verbal games are in truth the forbidden subject matter, the true object of repression. The poem installs a mocking idiolect of its own, made of phrases heard around, clandestine humor and enjoyment according to the strategy of survivors. In words of Perlongher:

> The poet writes verses which are not understood. This
> is because they operate the magic resource of their
> resonance in a different state of awareness, in a state
> of awareness close to trance the writer is submerged
> into, in which he writes, in which he aims to involve
> the reader, in which the reader is finally involved.

Ecstasy transliterates verbal resonance to build phrases by phonic association and wordplay.

> It looks for the intensive reverberation of sounds
> and colors, whispers and ideas… The ill-defined
> limits of the idea get bogged down in colorful
> dumps of whisper, murmur, mutter.

Our task as translators has been to determine the meanings of words and little phrases within their geopolitical field of resonance. It has also been to keep up their generating rhythm, the tautness of the verses, their economy and disposition, to keep them alive in a different language. We can't recreate the phonic associations that produced the original. But we can get the gist of its thought.

Roberto Echavarren & Donald Wellman

Roberto Echavarren is a poet, novelist, essayist and translator. Some of his books of poems are *Centralasia* (Ministry of Education and Culture of Uruguay Award, publications in Argentina, Mexico and Brazil), *El expreso entre el sueño y la vigilia* (The Expresso between Sleep and Wakefulness) (Nancy Bacelo Foundation Award) and *Ruido de fondo* (Background Noise). His essays include: *El espacio de la verdad: Felisberto Hernández* (The Space of Truth: Felisberto Hernández), *Arte andrógino* (Androgynous Art) (Ministry of Education and Culture of Uruguay Award), *Fuera de género: criaturas de la invención erótica*, (Beyond Gender: Creatures of Erotic Invention), *Michel Foucault: filosofía política de la historia*, (Michel Foucault: Political Philosophy of History), *Margen de ficción: poéticas de la narrativa hispanoamericana*, (Margin of Fiction: Poetics of Latin American Narrative). His novels are: *Ave roc*, *El diablo en el pelo* (The Devil in the Hair), *Yo era una brasa* (I Was an Ember), and *Archipiélago* (three short novels in one volume). His latest book of narrative, *Las noches rusas* (Russian Nights), is a chronicle about the political and cultural life of Russia in the twentieth century. He is director of La Flauta Mágica publishing company, specializing in critical bilingual editions of poetry and the rescue of major poetical works written in Spanish. Poetry books in English: *The Espresso between Sleep and Wakefulness* (Cardboard House Press, 2016), and *The Virgin Mountain* (Lavender Ink, 2017).

Donald Wellman is a poet and translator. He has translated books of poetry by Antonio Gamoneda, Emilio Prados, Yvan Goll, and Roberto Echavarren. *Albiach / Celan: Reading Across Languages* is from Annex Press (Spring 2017). His *Expressivity in Modern Poetry* is forthcoming from Fairleigh Dickinson University Press. His poetry has been described as trans-cultural and baroque. His collections include *Roman Exercises* (Talisman House, 2015), *The Cranberry Island Series* (Dos Madres, 2013), *A North Atlantic Wall* (Dos Madres, 2010), *Prolog Pages* (Ahadada, 2009), and *Fields* (Light and Dust, 1995). As editor of O.ARS, he produced a series of annual anthologies including *Coherence* (1981) and *Translations: Experiments in Reading* (1984).